D0097034

BETTY'S BOOK OF
LAUNDRY
SECRETS

BETTY FAUST and MARIA RODALE

RODALE

RODALE

WE INSPIRE AND ENABLE PEOPLE TO IMPROVE THEIR LIVES AND THE WORLD AROUND THEM

Editor: Jennifer Hornsby
Project Editor: Karen Bolesta
Interior Book Designers: Nancy Biltcliff and Marcella Bove-Huttie
Cover and Interior Illustrator: Barbara Pollak
Cover Designer: Michelle Raes
Layout Designer: Keith Biery
Copy Editor: Erana Bumbardatore
Manufacturing Coordinator: Jodi Schaffer
Indexer: Nanette Bendyna
Editorial Assistance: Kerrie A. Cadden

Rodale Organic Living Books
Executive Editor: Kathleen DeVanna Fish
Executive Creative Director: Christin Gangi
Art Director: Patricia Field
Content Assembly Manager: Robert V. Anderson Jr.
Studio Manager: Leslie M. Keefe
Copy Manager: Nancy N. Bailey
Director, Production Control/Rodale Products: Paul Snyder

Library of Congress Cataloging-in-Publication Data

Faust, Betty.
    Betty's book of laundry secrets / Betty Faust and Maria Rodale.
        p. cm.
    Includes index.
    ISBN 0–87596–933–X (alk. paper)
    1. Laundry. I. Rodale, Maria. II. Title.
    TT985 .F38 2001
    648'.1—dc21   2001002050

Distributed in the book trade by St. Martin's Press

2 4 6 8 10 9 7 5 3 1
paperback

We're always happy to hear from you. For questions or comments concerning the editorial content of this book, please write to

Rodale Book Readers' Service
33 East Minor Street
Emmaus, PA 18098

Look for other Rodale books wherever books are sold. Or call us at (800) 848-4735.

For more information about Rodale Organic Living magazines and books, visit us at

www.organicstyle.com

BETTY'S BOOK OF

LAUNDRY
SECRETS

For Rachel and Katie
and Maya and Eve

May you always remember Betty's secrets

contents

introducing Betty

Betty has seen a transformation in laundering.

Growing up on a farm in Pennsylvania in a family with eight kids, she helped do the laundry every Monday morning. Week after week, Betty and her mother carried the kettle out to the

yard, built a fire, filled the kettle with water, and washed the laundry with homemade soap. They always dried the laundry on an outdoor clothesline, and if the weather didn't cooperate, they would just move laundry day. Everything went through the wringer. Irons were really made of iron. Starch was cooked on the stove, and it scratched the heck out of your neck. That was just 70 years ago.

Times were different back then. They put clean clothes on every Saturday night, and they wore that one outfit all week. They slept two to a bed. They milked the cows every day before they walked to school. Back then, the boys never did the laundry. "They were farmers all the way," says Betty. How times have changed!

Now me, on the other hand—I'm a child of the '60s and '70s. I always say that the laundry gene skipped a generation with me. I do remember ironing my father's hankies when I was a kid and getting burned a few times by the iron. But mostly I remember being scolded for never picking up my clothes off the floor and for leaving them turned inside out. My mother was not liberated enough to make me do my own laundry, but she was liberated enough to be mad as hell about my sloppy habits. So I stayed as far away as possible from the washing machine when there was laundry to be done.

When I did finally have to do my own laundry, I earned a reputation for being wrin-

kled. When it came to laundry, I could do nothing right. What I needed then is what I have now—Betty. She's kind and she's tough. She gets the job done and done well, but she's not a fussy perfectionist who makes you feel inadequate. She's good-humored and resourceful, and she makes a delicious pumpkin pie. She's my hero.

I knew as soon as I met Betty that I had to write this book for all of you who need to do laundry but don't know how. It's simple. It's easy. Just follow her lead. Her life's laundry work and knowledge are collected in these brief but practical and inspiring pages.

Maria Rodale

Maria Rodale

1. stocking

Some basic supplies to make
the job easier

up

THOSE TV advertisements may make you think you need a whole room full of high-tech laundry supplies just to wash a pair of jeans, but there's really just a short list of things you will ever truly need.

Betty recommends just the basics to stock a laundry room. She is always trying the latest gadget or newest secret formula to see if it works. But here's what usually works best:

- Elbow grease
- Simple, quality products
- A bar of Ivory soap

laundry
room SUPPLIES

**Stock up on these supplies,
and doing laundry will be a breeze.**

- Bar of Ivory soap
- Powdered detergent
- Assorted plastic buckets for soaking clothes
- Scrub brush with plastic bristles
- Woolite or other mild liquid detergent
- Color-safe bleach
- Liquid fabric softener
- Cider vinegar
- Low-sided laundry baskets (they make it easy to load and unload clothes from the washer and dryer)
- Wooden clothespins
- Plastic-coated clothesline

- Plastic hangers
- Wire fold-out drying rack (wood gets warped and mildewed), unless you have a big backyard to fill with clotheslines

- Good-quality steam iron (unless, of course, you're aiming for the wrinkled look)

- Sturdy ironing board with a cotton cover

- Spray starch in spray bottle

- Scissors for clipping off threads and price tags

- Piggy bank or jar for collecting loose change

- Trash can for lint and assorted trash from pockets

Laundromat goers will also need:

- Lots of quarters

- Novels, magazines, and *Betty's Book of Laundry Secrets* to read during wash and dry cycles

2. sorting

What piles to make for
the best results

clothes

IMPROPER sorting is one of the most common mistakes a beginner can make, often leading to a wardrobe of clothes tinged with gray or stained from being washed with darker or brighter garments. And yet, sorting is simple—and it can even be satisfying, especially to those of you who like making neat little piles out of chaos.

Here are the top three benefits of good sorting practices:

- New clothes will look new longer.
- You will be less likely to destroy your favorite items.
- Whites will remain really white.

Basic Sorting Piles

It all starts with the piles. If you haven't had time to do the laundry for a week or more, it can feel as if those mile-high baskets of dirty socks and T-shirts are planning to topple your house. Having too much dirty laundry can be overwhelming, but you can take control with a little sorting. Great big piles of laundry can actually be a good thing because they allow you to do separate loads for different kinds of clothes and to wash, say, all your orange items together. Sort that small mountain of laundry into a few piles, and you'll restore order to your laundry baskets. Betty recommends sorting on the floor just before you're going to do your laundry. If your floor is made of wood, it's best not to let the piles sit for long because damp clothes or towels may stain the floor.

A Little Clarification

If you're still mystified by what goes into each pile, take heart. "Whites" are, well, pure white

Whites

Colors

Heavily soiled clothes

Hand-washables

Dry cleaning

Stained clothes

all over, with maybe a few T-shirt slogans in color. "Colors" make up a much broader category, with several subcategories. Generally, try to wash all like colors together: Pastels and creams can go together in one load; place medium blues, purples, and greens in another load; try washing reds, oranges, and pinks together; and dark colors can be washed together to avoid damaging lighter-color items. New Yorkers just need a black pile.

Sorting Piles	What to Do Next
Whites	Proceed to "Machine Washing" on page 44
Colors	Proceed to "Machine Washing" on page 44
Heavily soiled items and new clothes that might "bleed"	Proceed to "Soaking Clothes" on page 38
Hand-washables	Proceed to "Washing Delicates" on page 60
Dry cleaning	Proceed to "Dry & Wet Cleaning" on page 68, and then go to the dry cleaner
Clothes with "impossible" stains	Proceed to "Removing Stains" on page 26

The "Uh-Oh" Factor

You'll often come across a garment that won't easily fit into a category. You may have a load of blues and greens, a load of whites, a load of pastels—and one, odd bright yellow shirt that absolutely must be washed. Uh-oh.

When this happens, you'll have to decide: Is the shirt closer to pastel or closer to bright? If it's possible the shirt will ruin a whole load of lighter pastel clothes, take a risk with the single shirt by adding it to a load of darker colors. You'll probably wash those in cold water anyway, making the darker colors less likely to bleed on your bright yellow shirt.

Be especially careful when sorting these high-risk items:

●● New or nearly new clothes

●● Dark blue jeans

●● Brightly colored towels

●● Whites

●● Brightly colored clothes with white trim

Avoiding a Dye Bath

Items that may "bleed," or leach their dye into the water they're immersed in, include new and noncolorfast items. Some fabrics, such as denim, tend to bleed long after their first wash. A warning sign that something may bleed is a care label that says to wash the item with "like colors" or a label that says to wash alone in a small load. You can always test a new item by soaking it in a bucket of warm water to see if the water changes color. (Turn to page 44 to learn more.)

Isolating the Mess

The basic sorting principle of grouping like items together applies to types and degrees of soil as well as types of clothes. If mud-encrusted jeans are washed with a load of pastel T-shirts, the shirts may not get as clean as you'd like.

Heavily soiled items should be turned dirty side out so they are exposed to more abrasion against the water and other items in the washer. Baby clothing should be turned right side out because food stains are usually on the outside.

A Symbol Is Worth a Thousand Words, Maybe

Identify delicates, hand-washables, and dry-clean-only items by their care labels. The United States Federal Trade Commission requires that these labels be attached to clothing, but they only require manufacturers to list one "safe" method of cleaning the garment. These care labels may suggest a cleaning method that's explained only with symbols instead of words (many countries only use symbols on their care labels). To figure out what those little garment-care symbols mean, see the most common examples shown below.

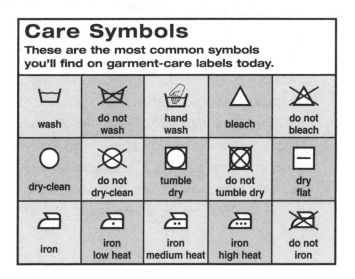

Care Symbols

These are the most common symbols you'll find on garment-care labels today.

wash	do not wash	hand wash	bleach	do not bleach
dry-clean	do not dry-clean	tumble dry	do not tumble dry	dry flat
iron	iron low heat	iron medium heat	iron high heat	do not iron

Avoiding Mishaps

Don't get caught with your zipper open! Open zippers will rub up against other clothes in the washer and dryer, making garments wear out more quickly. Zip up all zippers while you sort. Betty also recommends checking every garment pocket while you sort. Remove facial tissues, pens, change, and trash from pockets to prevent ruining a load of wash. Plus, you never know what treasures you'll find— from quarters to chocolate bars.

Another trick for avoiding problems is to keep fabrics that attract lint, such as flannels and synthetic fleece, separated from items that give off lint, such as new sweatshirts, terry cloth towels or robes, and that fuzzy wool blanket you keep in the trunk of your car in case of an emergency. If you don't separate these items, you may end up modeling a flannel shirt covered with bathrobe lint—not the sharpest look.

BETTY'S
wash-and-wear WISDOM

ALWAYS check the labels on new clothes to see what they say, but don't always believe them. Sometimes the manufacturers don't even sew on the right tag. A lot of clothes have labels that say dry-clean only, but many of these garments can actually be hand-washed. (See pages 60–67 for details on what to hand wash.)

3. removing

A bar of Ivory soap for everything

stains

BETTY is a genius at removing spots, from chocolate and grass to mildew and ink. But she doesn't put much faith in all those miracle potions you can buy at the super-market. She believes in two things: a bar of Ivory soap and a scrub brush.

The key to preventing a spot from becoming a permanent stain is treating it before it bakes in the dryer. Also, remember:

- ● Check your clothes for stains before washing them.

- ● Double-check before drying.

- ● When in doubt, soak spots in cold water.

The Ivory Soap Method

Think you're destined to walk around wearing marinara stains on the front of your shirt simply because you're not a professional laundress? Think again. Betty's favorite laundry trick may seem almost too easy, but it's certainly effective. Ivory soap works well because it's mild (with an almost-neutral pH) and it doesn't contain moisturizers, deodorants, and other unnecessary additives. Other mild white bar soaps will work, too, but save those colorful, moisturizer-laden, or highly perfumed soaps for unwinding in the bathtub. For stain removal, plain old soap works wonders.

1. Wet the stained garment with cold water.

2. Rub a bar of Ivory soap directly into the stain, then rinse.

3. If that doesn't remove the stain, rub Ivory soap on the stain again, and then soak the fabric for 30 minutes or so in cold water with a bit of powdered detergent dissolved in it. (If you forget and leave stuff soaking longer, it doesn't really matter; you won't hurt the fabric.) Rinse.

4. If that still doesn't work, rub more bar soap into the stain, scrub it with a scrub brush (taking care not to damage the fabric), and rinse.

5. If a second scrubbing attempt doesn't remove the stain, blot it gently with some color-safe bleach diluted with water, then rinse with clean water to remove all of the bleach.

6. If all else fails, be prepared to live with the stain.

Exceptions to the Ivory Soap Rule

Like most rules, there are exceptions. Certain stains require different methods of attack.

Coffee: Betty says that coffee isn't hard to get out if you get to it with soap and water right away.

Fruit: Betty always puts lemon on the stain first. If that doesn't work, then she uses bar soap.

Mildew: Wash the garment in warm or hot water with bleach, depending on the fabric (see page 49), and line-dry or dry flat in direct sunlight.

Oil and grease: Sprinkle some corn-starch or baking soda on the stain, then place the garment, stain side down, on a large rag on top of an ironing board. Iron with a hot iron on the wrong side of the stain—most oil and grease stains will come right out. (This trick works only for oil and grease, which need heat to dissolve.)

Rust: Soak fabric spotted with brown rust stains (which sometimes come from hard water) in a solution of 1 part lemon juice and 1 part water for at least 30 minutes. Do not use chlorine bleach on rust stains.

Tea stains: These are hard to get out, but Betty soaks tea stains in cool water and applies bar soap anyway.

Betty's Rules of Thumb for Stain Removal

●● Don't ever try to use hot water on anything that's stained. Hot water will set most stains, especially those containing protein (such as blood stains and many food stains).

●● When in doubt, soak it.

●● If you notice a stain on a garment after washing it, don't put it in the dryer. Instead, while the item is still damp, attack the stain with Ivory soap, as described on page 28.

●● If you catch a stain in the act—say, at a dinner party after one glass of wine too many—blot the stain immediately with a clean rag or sponge.

●● If a stain is faded but not completely gone after you take the garment out of the washer, hang the garment outside with the stain facing the sun. Often, sunlight will do the trick.

BETTY'S
wash-and-wear WISDOM

"A lot of those stain-removal products you can buy at the supermarket leave spots on clothes. You've got to keep an eye on those products really closely, or else they leave a mark from the bleach that's in them. Sometimes they even leave a hole. Ivory soap doesn't do that," Betty says.

"When I have stains, the first thing I use is cold water and a bar of Ivory soap. If that doesn't work, then I try again. Finally, I resort to diluted bleach. Sometimes I have to take extra measures. Usually I don't see all the stains 'til after I wash it. If I see one, I work on it and wash it again."

Don't give up on a stain too soon. If you find a new one even after you've washed a piece of clothing, try to get it out anyway. Lots of stains will come out even after they've been through the washing machine.

Preventing Stains

Some people are able to gracefully avoid stains. Others are magnets for stains and can't eat a simple snack without dripping spicy salsa or globs of chocolate ice cream down their shirtfronts. But most of us—at least, those of us who don't live with a 2-year-old child—can take precautions. Wear an apron when you're preparing messy foods and you'll save some spot-removal work. Change into old clothes before starting home-improvement projects. And even in a fancy restaurant, it's wise (if not chic) to wear a silly plastic bib when eating lobster.

Need the lowdown on avoiding those unsightly sweat stains that show up on the under-arms of T-shirts? Betty's preferred method is to line-dry the shirts outside. The combination of sunlight's natural bleaching properties and drying at lower temperatures than in a dryer keeps sweat stains from turning yellow. It's the heat of the dryer that sets the stains and makes them difficult to get out. If you insist on using the dryer all the time, wash clothes as quickly as you can after wearing; wear an undershirt, for land's sakes; and use Ivory soap and cool water or color-safe bleach to remove the stains.

Accidental bleaching is the opposite of a stain—it can't be taken out later because bleach removes color, so be extra careful when using any bleaching agents. Acne treatments that contain benzoyl peroxide will bleach fabrics they touch. If you use topical acne medicines, switch to white towels, face cloths, pillowcases, and top sheets. A much more obvious accidental bleaching product is, well, bleach—pour it carefully, and mop up any spills right away.

Stain Fighters

Betty relies on Ivory soap, the occa-
sional capful of color-safe bleach, and her trusty
scrub brush to remove the toughest stains, but
there are lots of other soil- and stain-removal products and brightening agents on the store
shelves. Here's a guide to making sense of them.

Enzymes. Most enzyme-based products
contain several different enzymes that attack
different types of stains. These products come
in either a spray bottle or a stick that you can dab
directly on the soiled item. Enzyme products work
best with presoaking.

Chlorine bleach. Chlorine bleach
can only be used on all-white items, but it's great
at restoring whiteness to dingy fabrics. Be careful
not to spill it or inhale the fumes, and wear gloves.
Chlorine bleach can harm certain fabrics, so
don't use it on cashmere, leather, mohair, nylon,
silk, spandex, or wool. To use, add it to the
washload with your detergent.

Color-safe bleach. Color-safe bleach, or oxygen bleach, is not as toxic or smelly as chlorine bleach, and it's often advertised as "environmentally safe." Wear gloves anyway, and add it to your washer with the detergent.

Bluing. Bluing is a brightener. Excessive bleaching will leave white fabrics with a yellowish tinge, which bluing can prevent. Some color-safe bleaches contain bluing agents already. Add bluing to the washer when you add the detergent.

Solvents. Some stain removers contain solvents. These products are toxic, but they're weaker than full-strength solvents, such as turpentine. Solvents attack stains that soap and water can't fix: ink, paint, fingernail polish, and indelible marker. To use a product with solvents, apply a dab directly to the stain, and scrub with a rag. Wear gloves, use in a ventilated area, and keep solvents away from heat sources. Rinse the item thoroughly, then launder it, and never put anything soaked in solvents in the dryer (solvents are flammable).

4. soaking

The lost art of soaking and
how it can make your life easier

clothes

ONE of Betty's best laundry secrets is soaking. She just throws soiled clothing into buckets of water, adds a little detergent (or whatever is called for), and lets the water loosen dirt and oils from clothes. Very dirty clothes will come clean in a cold-water wash cycle if they've soaked for an hour or so before they're laundered.

Soaking may seem old-fashioned, but it's a low-tech way to lessen your use of chemical laundry products. Soaking will:

- Remove tough stains.
- Rinse excess dye out of new clothes.
- Make doing laundry a breeze.

Soaking Basics

Betty has to have at least three buckets for soaking all sorts of things. She keeps these buckets by the laundry-room sink so they're easy to fill and empty.

If you don't have a laundry room, you can soak clothes in a bathroom sink, but be careful; fabrics can bleed their colors and stain your sink. It's best to use a bucket and to rinse the sink with clean water after washing any colorful water down the drain.

Dirty socks and underwear (yuck!):

Use warm water and half a cup of detergent with color-safe bleach. Then, if they don't get clean after soaking for an hour, use a scrub brush. Betty tries never to use chlorine bleach because she says "it makes clothes fall apart."

New clothes that might bleed:

If you have something new to be washed, put it in Woolite and cold water first, to see if it's going to bleed. If it does, wash it separately or with clothes that are the same color until it passes the colorfastness test. (See "Avoiding a Dye Bath" on page 22 for details.) The best way to keep colors from bleeding is to put a tablespoon of vinegar in the wash water. (Betty uses cider vinegar.) Put a little vinegar in your washing machine's rinse water, too.

Anything with tough stains:

Soak the clothing in a bucket of cool water for at least an hour. You could even soak heavily soiled clothes overnight if you aren't ready to wash them. Refer to "Removing Stains" on pages 26–37.

Bloodstains:

Anything with blood on it has to be soaked in cold water or the stain will set. (Try to rinse out blood as soon as the mishap occurs to make stain removal easier.) Rub some Ivory soap on the bloodstain, too. If a bloodstain has set and doesn't come out after the first wash, try using color-safe bleach on it.

Stained shirt collars: First wet
the collar with cold water to start to lift the stain.
Rub the soiled area of the collar with a bar of
Ivory soap. Then soak the shirt briefly in the
socks-and-underwear bucket, agitating the
water every so often, before throwing the shirt
in the wash.

To remove lipstick stains, follow the intructions
for removing oil and grease on page 30.

5. machine

It's as easy as 1, 2, 3

washing

MACHINE washers and dryers have eased the household workload. Modern washers are effective, fast, energy-efficient, easy to use, and nearly foolproof.

Just about any washing machine will get your clothes clean. But there are a few other considerations:

- Front-loaders use less water, electricity, and detergent.

- Top-loaders are less expensive up front but can cost more over the long haul.

- Washing machines need to be grounded; hire an electrician to do it.

Make It Simple

Machine-washing settings can seem mysterious to both the beginner and the experienced laundry-doer. The two most important variables you'll need to be aware of are the machine's setting and the temperature of the wash water.

Wash Settings

Most machines have the same four basic settings, although they aren't terribly different from each other, their names might make you think they are. Betty uses the normal cycle for almost everything she washes. She admits that "most of those buttons don't mean that much."

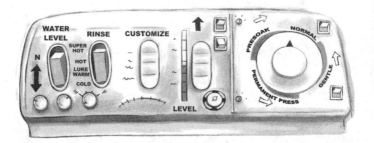

Normal: This cycle agitates your clothes for about 8 to 14 minutes, rinses them, then spins them around to remove water. This cycle is the best one for getting clothes clean.

Gentle or delicate: This cycle agitates your clothes more gently and for a shorter period of time, and it spins them more gently and for less time than the normal cycle. This cycle is recommended for washing knits, delicates, washable silks, acrylics, and rayons.

Permanent press: This cycle agitates your clothes for a shorter amount of time, but it agitates them more vigorously than they would be in the gentle cycle. Permanent press means an automatic cold-water rinse followed by a slow spin cycle. Manufacturers recommend this cycle for washing nondelicate synthetic fabrics such as polypropylene, polyesters, and blends.

Presoak: You can use the machine's pre-soak setting instead of soaking in a bucket.

Water Temperature

The hotter the water is, the harder it is on your clothes. Hot water (112° to 145°F, or 45° to 63°C) is better at killing germs and removing odors, but it causes stress on your clothes. Most items can be washed in cold water, but if you have bad allergies or are prone to illness, it might be worth it to wash your things in hot. (It takes hot water to terminate the mighty dust mite.) Warm water (87° to 111°F, or 31° to 44°C) kills more germs than cold water (anything at or below 86°F, or 30°C), but cold water and detergent will also kill most household germs.

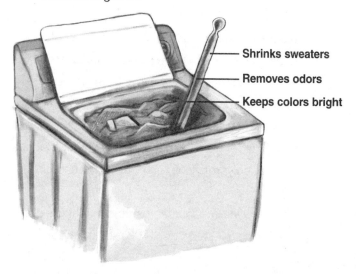

Shrinks sweaters
Removes odors
Keeps colors bright

Water Temperature and What to *Wash* in It

Hot water ●————● Anything that needs to be sterilized: germy handkerchiefs, underwear, cleaning rags, or the sheets and towels of a sick or allergic person

Warm water ●————● Polyesters, nylons, and color-safe light-colored clothes; smelly, color-safe workout clothes

Cold water ●————● Dark or brightly colored clothes and clothes that may shrink

Water Temperature and What to *Rinse* in It

Hot water ●————● Nothing

Warm water ●————● Nothing

Cold water ●————● Everything

Ready to Wash

This is the easy part: Set the dials to your chosen settings (such as cold wash, cold rinse, normal wash setting, and large load). Add powdered detergent as specified on the container. Betty prefers powdered detergent over liquid detergent because she says the powdered type "isn't as soap-scummy and won't leave a residue in your washing machine."

Close the lid of the washer, press or pull the start button, and allow a few inches of water to accumulate inside the machine—this way, your clothes won't have direct contact with undiluted detergent, which could cause fading. Open the lid, toss your clothes in loosely (without compacting them at all), and close the lid again. If your clothes come close to filling the washer, with just inches of room to spare, select the "extra-large load" setting. If they fill three-quarters of the tub, choose "large"; for one-half tub, choose "medium"; and for one-third tub, choose "small." That's it!

When you're confronted with a mountain of laundry, Betty recommends following her system:

●● First put in the loads that will need ironing. Then, while the other stuff is washing, you can do your ironing. Or if it's a nice day, do the stuff you want to put on the line first, so it has plenty of time to dry.

●● Rinse in cold water. "Why waste the hot water?" Betty wonders.

●● Some people say to wash everything in cold water, but Betty thinks it makes wrinkles set harder. Do not overload permanent press loads—there should be plenty of room for extra water to swish around the clothes so they wrinkle less.

●● Use fabric softener in the wash to take care of static cling.

●● To protect stockings, frilly underwear, and easy-to-lose items such as baby socks, place them in a mesh lingerie bag before tossing them in the washer.

Don't Go Overboard

Have you ever seen a washing machine shaking violently and acting, well, unbalanced? To prevent unbalanced loads, don't overload your washer. Clothes should be loaded loosely into the tub, and there should be several inches of space at the top. Leaving room for the water will not only help balance the load, but it will also ensure that your clothes come out clean and will reduce wrinkles.

Try to fill the washer with garments of different sizes and weights. A load full of blue jeans is more likely to become unbalanced than a mixed load of jeans, shirts, and smaller items. Try washing whole outfits in each wash cycle, not whole loads of a single type of garment.

Don't let damp clothes lie around in the washer for too long or they'll grow mildew and smell terrible (and then what's the point of washing them in the first place?). This happens especially fast when it's hot and humid. If this happens, wash them again.

BETTY'S
wash-and-wear WISDOM

BETTY says, "Be thankful for progress. We used to have big wooden washers, and at first they ran with a motor, like generators. But it wasn't a generator; this was a motor that you had to start and you had to put gas in, then it went putt, putt, putt.

"While I was growing up, we never had an automatic. We had a tub with a wringer and a tub for rinsing. It was all outside. Even when I got married, I didn't have an automatic. The first automatic washer I had was back in 1969. And soon after that the gas dryers came out.

"Would I ever wish to go back to those days? No! I think it was colder back then than it is today. We would stand out on the back porch all day—I don't remember what kind of coats we had, but they weren't *that* warm."

Surviving the Laundromat

Not everyone is lucky enough to have tons of space and a well-equipped laundry room. Apartment dwellers, students, and city folk alike know that visiting a coin-op laundry can be fun—or frustrating.

Following these tips will help and will clear more time for people-watching, reading a magazine, playing cards, or doing whatever you do to pass the time while your whites get whiter.

●● Avoid coin-op laundries that have bars and smoking areas in them—unless you love the smell of stale beer and cigarettes. The odors you'll find there will cling to your clothes until you wash them again.

●● Look out for drips and puddles of liquid on all surfaces. Innocent-looking wet spots may really be bleach in disguise—not something you want to get on your favorite black shirt.

●● No one's as careful as they should be. Inspect inside all washers and dryers before loading your clothes into them. Watch out for fresh pen ink, paper, tissues, and wads of dryer-baked chewing gum.

●● Start your washers and dryers in staggered shifts so they don't all finish at the same time.

●● Bring hangers with you, and hang up wrinkle-prone items such as dress shirts as soon as you take them out of the dryer.

●● Unless you like crowds, avoid doing laundry on weekends. Try Tuesday nights, instead.

●● If the washing machines you use have trouble rinsing all the suds out of your clothes, add half a cup of vinegar to the washers at the beginning of the rinse cycle. Vinegar will help neutralize soapy water.

●● Always bring more quarters than you think you'll need. Shifty quarters have a way of rolling into the tiny crack between two machines.

Earth-Friendly Detergents

There are a lot of decisions you need to make when choosing which detergents and concoctions you'll use to clean your clothes. Many laundry products are really toxic, even cancer-causing, but there are others that are safer for both you and the environment.

Your local grocery, discount, or health food store may carry powders and detergents that do not have irritating dyes and synthetic fragrances, so choose these products when they're readily available. The following products may contain petroleum, but they are still relatively gentle:

- All Free and Clear
- Ivory Snow
- CheerFree
- Liquid Woolite Cold Water Wash

If you're willing to go the extra mile to search out alternative laundry products, here's a list of the best environmentally safe clothes-cleaning supplies, none of which contains petroleum products. Many of these brands make powdered and liquid detergents, as well as soap-based cleaners and color-safe bleaches.

●● Bi-O-Kleen Premium Plus Laundry Powder. All-natural ingredients. Washes up to 50 loads per 5-pound box.

●● Cal Ben Seafoam Laundry Cleaner. All-natural laundry powders and liquid laundry soaps available.

●● Dr. Bronner's Sal Suds. Pure castile bar and liquid soaps available.

●● Earth Rite Liquid Laundry Detergent. Available in 64-ounce bottles.

●● Ecos Laundry Detergent. Concentrated laundry detergent includes built-in soy-based fabric softener and cellulose-based optical brightener. Available in liquid or powder.

•• Ecover Natural Laundry Powder.
Variety of laundry products available. Ecover
has been elected to the United Nations
"Global 500 Roll of Honor" for outstanding
environmental achievement.

•• EnviroRite Laundry Detergent.
Developed especially for people with allergies,
asthma, and chemical sensitivities. Free of
petroleum solvents, fragrances, and dyes.

•• Equator Low-Sudsing
Biodegradable Laundry
Detergent. Concentrated low-sudsing
detergent was designed for front-loading
machines but can be used in top-loaders, too.

•• Seventh Generation Free and
Clear Natural Laundry Detergent.
Fragrance free with no brighteners, bleaches,
or animal testing.

●● Sodasan Compact Laundry
Powder and Liquid Laundry
Detergent. **Laundry products only
contain ingredients derived from certified
organic agriculture.**

●● Sun and Earth Ultra Laundry
Detergent. **This hypoallergenic liquid
detergent is made from palm and coconut
oils and is 100 percent biodegradable.
on the environment. Has a citrus scent but
contains no added perfumes, preservatives,
or dyes. No animal testing.**

If you can't find any of these products in
your local supermarket, try shopping at a
health food store, ordering by mail, or
even buying from an Internet source. Refer
to "Green Laundry Products" on page 122 for
information on other companies that sell
earth-friendly products.

6. washing

How not to shrink a sweater

delicates

ONE of the more intimidating laundry tasks is hand washing delicate garments. It doesn't have to be nerve-wracking, although mistakes can and do happen. If you're worried about or have paid a lot for a sweater or other garment, take the safe route and dry-clean it. But for most hand-washables, you'll be happy to know that all you need is a little courage and a light touch.

Here are some prime candidates for hand washing:

- Bras and other delicate lingerie
- Most sweaters
- Hand-embroidered items

The Basics of Hand Washing

Determining what to throw in the washer, what to dry-clean, and what to hand-wash is usually quite easy: You just read the garment-care label and follow the label directions. (See page 23 for more information on care labels.) Some people find themselves rereading garment-care labels each time they do laundry, but most folks will develop a feel for what's machine-washable, what's hand-washable, and what must be dry-cleaned. When the label's missing or just doesn't seem right, you have to use your judgment.

To Hand-Wash or Not to Hand-Wash

Betty recommends washing most suspicious fabrics by hand, except for anything that's lined. Lined garments, tailored or fine wool items, and nubby or very delicate silks should always be dry-cleaned. Some items can be hand washed but require such careful treatment that you may prefer to have them dry-cleaned. Cashmere sweaters, for example, can easily develop pills if they're treated at all roughly in the hand-washing process. After a few minor accidents, you'll find that the best way to get the most out of your investment is to send anything made of cashmere to the dry cleaner.

Type of Clothing or Bedding	Best Washing Method
Sweaters	Wash in a bucket with cold water and Woolite for about 3 minutes. Rinse in cold water. Dry flat.
Most silks	Wash in the machine on the gentle cycle. Hang to dry.
Washable rayon	Wash in the machine on the gentle cycle. Hang to dry.
Pantyhose	Wash in a bucket with cold water or in the machine on the gentle cycle in a mesh bag. Hang to dry.
Lingerie	Wash in a bucket with cold water or in the machine on the gentle cycle in a mesh bag. Hang to dry.
Pillows	Wash in the machine on the gentle cycle. Put them in the dryer with a clean tennis ball to fluff them.
Comforters	Wash in warm water in a large, front-loading machine. Tumble-dry on low with a couple of clean tennis balls to fluff them.

How to Hand-Wash

Hand washing is even simpler than machine washing (and Betty says it's even a whole lot more fun).

1. Run cool water into a bucket or sink.

2. Add Woolite or another mild detergent designed for washing delicates, as specified on the bottle.

3. If you don't have any Woolite handy and need to hand-wash in a pinch, you can improvise with baby shampoo or dishwashing liquid (not automatic dishwasher detergent).

4. Submerge the garment.

5. Swish it gently in the wash water for about 3 minutes.

6. Drain the water, rinse the item thoroughly, and dry it flat or on the line, according to the fabric type.

After Hand Washing

To dry a sweater, roll it up in a towel to absorb the extra moisture and then lay it flat. You have to stretch the sweater out as it's drying; otherwise it will shrink right up. Lay it out flat on a work surface, and stretch it gently into the right shape. Dry it flat on a mesh sweater dryer (a screen that fits over the bathtub for drying items flat) or on a towel draped over a collapsible drying rack. See page 80 for tips on hanging less-delicate items, either on an inside or outside clothesline.

BETTY'S
wash-and-wear WISDOM

MOST silks are labeled "dry-clean only," but you may want to experiment and see if you can avoid the high cost of dry cleaning. If a garment is unlined and not too fancy, it will probably hand-wash really well.

Breaking the Rules

Some garments are labeled to be washed by hand but can really be done in the machine. The only way to know for sure is to try it. Sometimes you can throw hand-washables in the washer toward the end of a rinse cycle (after you've washed them in a bucket). They rinse better in the washer than if you were to rinse them by hand. In general, the less you paid for something, the more you can take a risk on washing it. Use common sense, though, and be more careful about washing the clothes you dearly love.

7. dry & wet

When to follow—and when to ignore—those garment-care labels

cleaning

BETTY doesn't buy anything that she can't wash herself—but other people sure do. Betty recommends avoiding dry cleaning as much as you can. Buying clothes you can wash yourself is the best way to save on dry-cleaning bills.

These days, many business and dress clothes are labeled "dry-clean only." While office-casual dress codes and the availability of washable silks, linens, and rayons means that you can wash most of your clothes yourself, there's still a need for dry cleaning. If you want to clean that interview suit or little black dress, you'll probably find yourself paying a visit to your local dry cleaner.

Dry versus Wet

Dry cleaning has been around for ages, but professional wet cleaning is a relatively new procedure that's popped up in many areas of the country, especially those attuned to environmental issues. But what's the difference between these two cleaning processes, and how do you choose? Read on to find out!

Dry Cleaning

Dry cleaning is a process using detergents and chemical solvents such as perchloroethylene (the most commonly used solvent) to clean and deodorize fabrics. Professional dry cleaners also use steam on and press certain fabrics. Both dry-cleaning solvents and steaming kill germs and remove soil and stains, and the goal of most dry cleaners is to make clothing look, feel, and smell as good as new.

It may sound like a wonderful invention, but there are downsides to the squeaky-clean world of dry cleaning. It's expensive. It can leave supposedly clean clothes smelling like the solvents used to clean them. And if solvents are not handled properly, dry cleaning can be toxic—both to the environment and to dry cleaners' employees (perchloroethylene has been identified as a possible carcinogen by the U.S. Food and Drug Administration).

Wet Cleaning

In the 1990s, wet cleaning gained popularity. Wet cleaning—which is sometimes nicknamed "green cleaning"—is a process that means the professional laundering of somewhat-delicate fabrics. Professional cleaners use special equipment and detergents to safely clean garments without shrinking, stretching, or discoloring them.

BETTY'S
wash-and-wear WISDOM

DON'T forget to pick up the dry cleaning! Keep those easy-to-lose dry-cleaner's tickets stashed in your wallet or in a safe place in your car. That way, they're easy to get your hands on when it comes time for you to pick up your clothes.

If you are really not sure about how to clean a garment, give in and take it to the dry cleaner. Sometimes it's best not to take chances.

Wet cleaning is considered better for the environment, as there are no solvent by-products being released into the air and no used solvents to dispose of. Not all fabrics can be wet-cleaned, though, so cleaners who use this process must either dry-clean these delicate items or send them out to a wholesale dry cleaner. Items that aren't wet-cleanable include garments prone to excessive bleeding or fading, very shrink-prone fabrics, and items with stains that are not water-soluble, such as wax.

Aftercare

Chemical odors can get trapped inside those plastic dry-cleaning bags. Take the plastic off right away and let the clothes air out in a well-ventilated area. Leaving the clothes wrapped in plastic will not allow dry-cleaning chemicals and fumes to escape your newly cleaned clothing and could be potentially toxic to the wearer. Also, extended contact with plastic dry-cleaning bags can cause your clothes to yellow.

What to Dry-Clean

If you follow the directions on garment-care labels, chances are you'll be patronizing your dry cleaner often. The truth is that the "dry-clean" label means only that a garment can be dry-cleaned. "Dry-clean only" is a stronger recommendation, and it means that the manufacturer believes that dry cleaning is the best method of cleaning the garment. Dry cleaning is the easiest and safest way to get some garments clean—but it's rarely the most cost-effective method, and it's usually harsh on the environment.

Before dropping off clothes at the dry cleaner, inspect them. If you see any stains, make sure to show them to your dry cleaner. If you can, tell them what caused the stain so they will know which chemical to use on it. If you're not sure whether to risk hand washing something with a "dry-clean" label, ask yourself if you'd mind much if the garment shrank or bled. If the answer is yes, or if you paid a lot of money for the garment, you probably want to dry-clean it rather than wash it.

What to dry-clean:

●● Anything lined

●● Really special or fragile items

●● Any sweater or other item that you absolutely never want to shrink

●● Cashmere items that you'd like to keep free of "pills" (washing cashmere by hand makes it much fuzzier than having it dry-cleaned)

●● Wool or down jackets, vests, and coats

●● Items that are too large to fit into your washing machine

●● Garments with "dry-clean only" labels

What to try washing by hand:

●● Unlined fabrics that you usually wash (such as cotton, silk, or acrylic)

8. drying

It's always best on the line

clothes

BETTY will do anything to hang clothes on the line all year-round. According to her, "It's just better that way." On one icy, snowy day, Betty rigged up an upside-down garbage can, a picnic bench, and an old skid as a set of steps leading down to the lawn from the first-floor window.

Rather than going out the side door and walking through the yard to get to the clothesline, she had been taking the short-cut out the window. And this at age 73! "It was easier than shoveling the walk," she said without remorse.

Line-Drying

According to Betty, there are only two times to use a dryer—when it's raining outside and when the clotheslines are full and you still have drying to do. Clothes can dry on the line even when it's freezing outside. Everything dries better on the line, and line-dried clothes end up smelling like fresh air. There is absolutely no substitute for sinking your head into a freshly dried pillow or drying yourself briskly with a line-dried towel. And there's an added bonus: Small doses of sunshine will keep your whites bleached whiter—when you have sun, that is!

Betty says that putting your clothes in the dryer all the time will make them turn yellow from the combination of heat and perspiration. Hanging clothes on the line will keep them looking their best, as long as they don't remain in direct, bright sunlight all day long. Too much direct sunlight (more than a few hours) can discolor your clothes, so leave your clothes in the sun just long enough for them to dry completely.

White clothes and towels take longer to dry on the line than dark clothes and towels do, since white reflects the sunlight and dark colors absorb it. If you're going to dry clothes on the line, do the whites first so they have more time to dry.

Betty's Best Bets

Betty recommends that the novice clothesline user follow these foolproof suggestions:

●● Use a plastic-coated clothesline rather than a rope one. If you want to keep the rope ones clean, you need to take them down after the laundry is dry and rehang them on the next laundry day. Rope clotheslines absorb lots of moisture (which becomes mildew over time) and attract dirt (which can soil your clothes when you hang them to dry).

●● Before you hang your clothes out on the plastic clothesline, wipe it off with a warm, wet cloth to remove all the dirt.

●● Use wooden clothespins (the kind with springs) instead of plastic ones. Plastic ones slide too much and don't grip clothes tightly enough.

●● Pair up your clothesline and dryer to get fast, fresh, wrinkle-free garments. If you take clothes out of the dryer while they are still damp, you can brush the wrinkles right out of them with your hand. Betty says that ironing T-shirts takes the freshness out of them, so she puts them in the dryer for 10 minutes, smoothes the wrinkles out, and then hangs them outside to finish drying.

●● Take hangers outside with you when you're ready to take dress shirts and blouses off the clothesline. You'll save a few minutes of ironing at the very least, and you might not have to iron at all!

●● Have enough laundry baskets at the ready, and don't overload them with folded clothes. Piling folded clothes too high is a recipe for wrinkles.

●● Take time to enjoy the fresh outdoor air.

It's a Fine Line

When hanging clothes on a line, be sure to attach the clothes in the smoothest way possible.

1. Using plenty of clothespins, clip the garments onto the line at their seams.

2. To avoid the dents and creases that clothespins can sometimes leave on a heavy garment, try to attach heavy items in spots where a little dent won't show.

3. Fold larger items, such as sheets, before pinning them up. You can fold a sheet in half, joining the top and bottom edges, and pin the edges to the clothesline to avoid any large creases and to keep the sheet from dragging on the ground.

Indoor Drip-Drying

If you don't have an extra room to set up a clothesline indoors, you can hang up wet clothes on hangers and let them dry from a bathtub curtain rod. Use plastic rather than metal hangers to hang things dry; you'll avoid accidental rust stains and you'll get softer creases and drying lines. Or set up a clothesline in a spare room or basement— just make sure to turn on a dehumidifier if it's damp.

Machine Drying

Most clothes can be dried safely in an automatic dryer, but anything made of polypropylene or rubber should be hung to dry. Some fabrics, such as spandex, viscose, acetate, Lycra, and acrylic, can be dried in the dryer, but they will last much longer and will not shrink if you hang them to dry.

Garments made of these fabrics usually have care labels that warn against putting them in the dryer, so be sure to take notice of what the label says.

Dryer Settings

Dryers have even more confusing dials than washers, but here are the basics.

Permanent Press: In this cycle, the dryer cools down for a while before stopping, keeping clothes from getting too wrinkled.

Air-Fluff: Most dryers also have this setting, which will slowly dry clothes with room-temperature air and no heat. This is best for articles containing rubber (which may melt) or for fluffing up damp knit fabrics that are prone to shrinking.

Normal: This option often includes the settings "Less Dry" and "More Dry." Most garments can be dried on the automatic, or normal, setting, which electronically detects how dry your clothes are and times itself according to the amount of moisture left. Most dryer dials have a range from "Less Dry" to "More Dry." Pick "Less Dry" if you're planning to iron the load. If not, choose something closer to "More Dry." Items that should be set on "More Dry" include thick towels, jeans, and thick cotton socks. An easy, energy-efficient way to dry a load is to set the dial halfway between the two settings.

Successful Machine Drying

When transferring clothes from washer to dryer, remove anything that shouldn't be dried, such as underwire bras, synthetic workout clothes, panyhose, lace tablecloths, delicate scarves, nylon slips, plastic-coated bibs, or wool socks.

Apply the same sorting principles you used before you washed your clothes: Don't dry light-colored items with noncolorfast items, and avoid combining linty garments (such as new towels) with items that attract lint (such as corduroys, sweatshirts, and velour).

BETTY'S
wash-and-wear WISDOM

DON'T forget to take the lint out of the dryer's lint screen before starting each new dryer load.

Follow Betty's machine-drying tips for best results:

●● If you can't hang wet clothes out on the line, dryer sheets do a decent job of making clothes smell fresh. They're still not as good as hanging clothes outside on the line, though!).

●● You can often reuse dryer sheets a second time and still get great results.

●● Fill your dryer about one-third full. Overloaded dryers will work slowly and cause wrinkles.

●● Avoid back strain by using a low-sided laundry basket. You can park the basket right in front of the dryer door to load and unload the clothes, and you'll find you're bending less often.

●● If you've let clothes sit in the dryer for too long, wet a washcloth, toss it in the dryer, and send the clothes for another spin. That little bit of moisture is often enough to get out any wrinkles.

Laundromat Drying

Most coin-operated laundry dryers operate on a strict quarter-per-time-period basis. You'll probably need about 30 minutes to dry most loads. The normal setting on most industrial dryers is very hot, so you're better off not machine-drying anything that's the least bit delicate. Clothes tend to shrink and wear more quickly if they're consistently dried in hot, coin-operated laundry dryers. Rubber waist-bands wear out more quickly, too, and knitted sweaters and vests seem to lose their elasticity.

When transferring clothes to the dryer, set aside anything that's not cotton. Place synthetic items in a separate dryer that's set to permanent press or a low-heat setting— or even better, take them home still wet and hang them to dry on a folding rack. Hanging them to dry will save you some quarters and some waiting-around time.

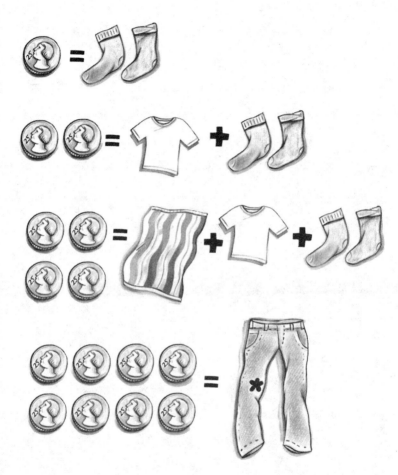

**What Might Dry with a Handful
of Quarters in a Coin-Op Dryer**

9. ironing

Secrets to wrinkle-free living

clothes

IT was 98°F in the room, and Betty was ironing. She wore an ice pack around her neck, but she was still dripping with sweat. I tried to convince her to stop; just watching her iron was making me warm, so she must have been sweltering. But Betty was a trouper, as usual: "This isn't nearly as hot as being out in the hot sun and having to throw hay up onto a hay wagon. That's hot."

Ironing is easier than it looks, if you know Betty's basic rules:

- •• Iron clothes when they're damp.
- •• Using starch is a matter of taste.
- •• Turn up the steam.

Successful Ironing

Even to a professional laundress, ironing can be "a really big pain." But Betty says she loves it. That's because she's figured out how to do it right. From the start, she recommends that you buy the best iron you can afford to make the job easier. Use a large ironing board with a smooth, padded cover. Betty's advice: "Cotton ironing board pads with cotton covers are the best since they absorb some of the moisture."

Betty's key to ironing is to not let clothes get too dry before she irons them. If you don't have time to iron soon after removing semidamp clothes from the dryer or clothesline, you can try this time-honored trick: Roll the damp garments tightly and wrap them in a plastic bag. Store the plastic bag in the freezer to avoid growing mildew on your newly washed clothes. If you'll have time to iron within a half-day of rolling and chilling, the refrigerator is cold enough to keep clothes fresh and odor-free.

The heat of the iron—not how hard you press down with it—is what takes out wrinkles. Use a lightweight iron in a size that's comfortable in your hands, and save your wrists some extra work. Gently glide the iron over the surface of the fabric; there's no point in pressing down hard on the clothes.

Start with ironing clothes that take the coolest iron, and then work your way to the hot-iron clothes, such as cottons and linens. Most irons have very clear temperature keys printed on them; these keys usually recommend using a cool or low setting for synthetic fabrics, a warm or medium setting for wool and silk, and a hot or high setting for cotton and linen.

Point of iron

Water fill

Iron Care

Betty drains the water out of the iron when she's done ironing, and then she lets the iron dry out. "If the water sets in there, it's liable to corrode. And if it gets into those little pores, the water turns dark, and you can get stains that way. I don't bother using distilled water. But I use a lot of water when I iron, and a lot of steam. Before I know it, the water is all gone. I always use steam when I iron."

Betty says that the easiest fabrics to iron are cotton and rayon blends and silk, while the hardest is heavy cotton, such as a thick tablecloth or a casual shirt.

BETTY'S
wash-and-wear WISDOM

TAKE clothes out of the dryer before they are completely dry; they are much easier to iron that way. Or you can hang them to see if the wrinkles will fall right out without out even being touched by an iron.

Ironing a **Shirt**

Start by ironing the cuffs, then move on to the yoke (the fitted part at the top of the shoulders). Iron the collar next, starting at the outside edges and moving inward, then do the sleeves. After that, iron the front, then the back. You usually have to touch up the sleeves again—they often get wrinkled while you iron the rest of the shirt. You can use a mini–ironing board on the sleeves to iron them more easily. Use small strokes for smaller parts of the shirt, such as the collar, to avoid adding new wrinkles with your iron.

Ironing **Pants**

Unzip or unbutton pants and turn them inside out, then iron around the waistband at the top of the pants. Iron the insides of the pockets. Then turn the pants right side out and iron the outside. Betty likes to fold and crease the pants. "Pants iron the easiest of anything. I put the seams together and shake them real well. Then I match up the seams."

Ironing Silks and Rayons

Some fine silks and rayons will develop a shiny look if they're ironed too roughly at a high temperature. You can use a store-bought pressing cloth on these fabrics, or you can improvise: Lay the article on a towel. Place a cut-up T-shirt, thin dish towel, or man's handkerchief over the garment to create a homemade pressing cloth. Iron at a low to medium setting. If wrinkles remain, dampen the pressing cloth and try again.

Ironing around Buttons

To iron around buttons, you'll need an iron with ridges around its sides, near the soleplate (the bottom of the iron). These ridges fit under buttons and make it easy to iron around them. Iron the back side of the article first, without ironing over the buttons. Then turn it over and iron around the buttons.

Ironing Difficult Items

There's a reason that professional dry cleaners charge so much; ironing suits and sport coats is hard work. If you need to touch up a tricky item, you can try ironing at a low temperature on the back side of the garment, using a pressing cloth. Dampen the cloth if this doesn't work. You can also purchase a hand-held steamer for touching up delicates and dress clothes, but be careful not to burn your fingers. If you need to do more than just touch up a wrinkled suit, let the professionals do what they do best.

To Starch or Not to Starch

Some people like the crisp look and feel of a starched cotton, cotton-blend, or linen garment—usually a shirt. Others dislike that same crisp feeling, preferring the softer feel of unstarched cotton. Whether you choose to use starch or not should be based entirely on preference, though starching your shirts will help maintain a neat, somewhat glossy, wrinkle-free look.

Starch Roulette

There are three types of starch—liquid starch, dry starch, and spray starch.

•• Liquid starch is added to the washing machine during the final rinse cycle, but if you use liquid starch, you must sort your loads even more carefully; everything in the washer will come out starched. Betty recommends using liquid starch if you want something—such as, a decorative linen hand towel—to be really, really stiff and wrinkle-free. She uses spray starch for shirts and other woven cotton garments.

•• Dry starch is spray starch that you make at home by adding water to it in a spray bottle according to package directions. With dry starch, you can control the concentration of your starch and make it "starchier," if you like. To use either store-bought or home-mixed spray starch, spritz your garment with the starch before ironing. You may want to turn the iron down a little lower than usual because starch can scorch and turn brown if it's too hot.

•• Spray starch comes in a spray bottle and often contains additives that make the iron glide more easily. It doesn't flake the way liquid starch does.

After ironing with starch, you can clean the bottom of your iron with a mixture of baking soda and warm water. You can also buy a commercial soleplate cleaner at hardware or fabric stores. Use a soft brush or plastic dish scrubber to remove excess starch and mineral buildup, and wipe the iron clean with a damp sponge. Starch buildup can scorch, causing brown spots to rub off on items while you iron them.

BETTY'S
wash-and-wear WISDOM

DON'T forget to turn off the iron and unplug it when you're done. Or, if you have trouble remembering to turn it off, buy an iron that turns itself off after it sits idle for a few minutes.

10. folding

A complete guide for those of
us who haven't worked in a Gap

laundry

GOOD folding intentions have often ended up in heaps and crinkled piles. But if you learn to fold well, you can spend much less time at the ironing board, while still looking smooth and wrinkle-free. The goal of folding is to get the creases in inconspicuous places.

Betty has a helpful trick or two up her (neatly folded) sleeve:

- Fold as soon as clothes come out of the dryer.

- Use a flat surface, such as a table or bed, to fold on.

- Fold—don't hang—knits to avoid hanger creases.

Flawless Folding

A good folding job means the difference between a dresser full of wrinkle-free, ready-to-wear clothes and a dresser full of clothes that need to be ironed—again.

Folding a T-Shirt

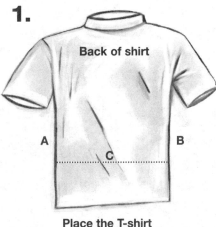

1.

Back of shirt

A   C   B

Place the T-shirt
face down.

2.

B

**Fold sides A
and B in toward
each other.**

3.

C

**Fold the bottom
of the T-shirt up
at line C.**

Folding a
Long-Sleeve Shirt

1.

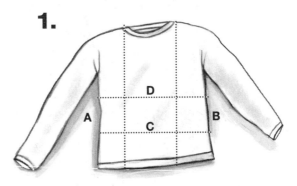

Place the long-sleeve
shirt face down.

2.

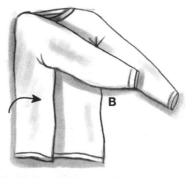

Fold side A in toward
the middle.

3.

Fold the side A sleeve back
toward the edge of the shirt.
Repeat for side B.

4.

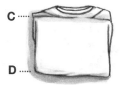

Fold the bottom
of the shirt up
at lines C and D.

Folding Pants
with a Crease

1.

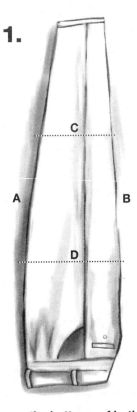

2.

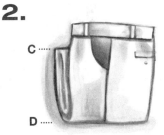

**Fold the pants
in thirds at lines
C and D.**

**Grasp the bottoms of both
legs and hang the pants
upside down. Match inseams
and crease lines A and B. Use
your hands to press the pant
legs together.**

Folding Pants
without a Crease

1.

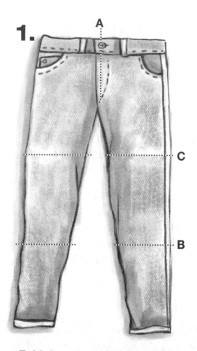

Fold the pants right down
the middle at line A;
do not press.

2.

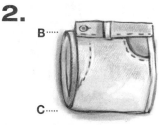

Fold the pants
in thirds at lines
B and C.

Rolling **Socks**

1.

Lay one sock on
top of the other.

2.

Start at the toe
and roll upward.

3.

At the top, open
up the outside
sock and pull it
over the roll.

BETTY'S
wash-and-wear WISDOM

DON'T forget to put your clothes away
after they're washed, dried, and folded—
they'll stay cleaner and less wrinkled than
if they're stacked in the laundry basket.

Folding a **Towel**

1.

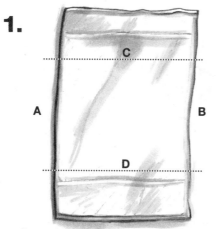

Spread the towel out on a flat surface.

2.

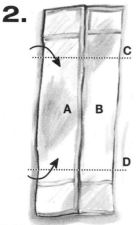

Fold sides A and B in toward each other until they meet.

3.

Fold the towel toward the center at line C, then fold toward the center again at line D.

Folding a Fitted Sheet

1.

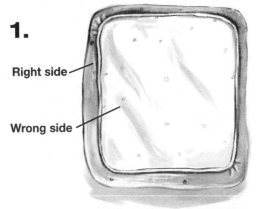

Right side

Wrong side

Hold the sheet from its corners
with the right side of the
corners facing you.

2.

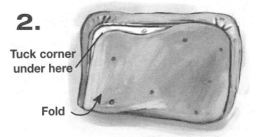

Tuck corner
under here

Fold

Fold the sheet across the
middle, tucking one set of
corners into the other.

3.

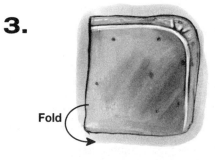

Fold

Smooth out wrinkles, then fold
the sheet in half in the other
direction, stacking corners on
top of corners.

4.

Fold

Fold the sheet in
half again.

Maria's Packing Tips

Betty doesn't travel much, but lots of folks do, and most of us have arrived at a destination or two with a suitcase full of mashed-up, wrinkled clothes (with the hope that the hotel has a decent iron). Try these packing tips to help your clothes stay fresh-looking on trips.

- •• Roll clothes rather than folding them. They are less likely to get wrinkled.

- •• When you arrive, unpack right away and hang everything up. Sometimes you can hang clothes in a steamy bathroom to get out minor wrinkles.

- •• Choose and pack clothes that don't wrinkle easily.

- •• Take a big plastic bag or a spare bag to put all of your dirty laundry in so you are not mixing dirty clothes with clean ones as you go.

- ●● Select travel clothes that don't weigh a lot.

- ●● Pack clothes in garment bags. They really do keep suits and dresses looking fresh.

- ●● Keep your toiletries in a plastic bag to avoid leaks and stains. Better yet, carry your toiletry bag in your carry-on bag when flying.

- ●● Put your shoes in bags so they don't soil your clothing by rubbing up against them.

BETTY'S
wash-and-wear WISDOM

HANG as many items as you can fit in your closet, so you'll have less folding to do. But don't overdo it—squashing as many clothes as you can fit into a closet will only cause wrinkles. Clothes should hang with some space around them.

Storing Clothes

After you've gone through all the trouble of washing, drying, and ironing clothes, what can you do to store items that you wear less frequently? Maybe you have childhood memories of sweaters that looked great but reeked of mothballs. Sure, there were no moth holes, but did you really want to wear a sweater that smelled of paradichlorobenzene? Mothballs, which can also be made of naphthalene, are toxic and should not be used in clothing storage.

There are less-smelly ways to keep your clothes safe from pests:

●● Hang suits, dresses, and blazers in a closet, and protect them inside heavyweight, zippered canvas bags.

●● Buy zippered sweater bags, and store sweaters inside them. Keep sweater bags in a chest, closet, or another safe, low-humidity spot.

●● Do not store clothes in a humid basement.

●● To keep clothes smelling fresh, tuck sachets in your drawers and clothing-storage bags. Use moth-repelling herbal sachets or cedar blocks instead of mothballs; your nose will be grateful when you wear the clothes.

Betty's
pumpkin
pie

The ultimate Thanksgiving stain-maker

What's a pumpkin pie recipe doing in a laundry book? Every year at Thanksgiving, Betty brings me a pumpkin pie. No matter what fancy recipes I try when making my own "gourmet" pie, my husband says (and I agree) that Betty's tastes better. A good pie is a good pie.

Life is filled with hard work and tasks that need doing, but when it's all said and done, the best things are simple and shared with family and friends. These things usually involve food. And food usually involves making a mess! Use your favorite pie crust recipe or a store-bought crust. Canned pumpkin will work fine, but here's a tasty way to use real pumpkin.

To prepare fresh pumpkin, cut open a medium-size pumpkin and scoop out the seeds. Cut the remaining pumpkin into quarters, place the pieces skin-side-down on a cookie sheet, and bake in the oven at 350°F (180°C) until the pumpkin is soft. Remove it from the oven, let it cool, and scoop out the fruit.

For a rough texture, mash fruit by hand and do the mixing by hand, too. For a smooth texture, puree it in a blender or food processor and use an electric mixer.

2 tablespoons butter	¼ teaspoon cinnamon
¾ cup sugar	½ teaspoon nutmeg
2 eggs	1½ cups mashed pumpkin
½ teaspoon salt	1½ cups milk

Preheat the oven to 375°F (190°C). In a large mixing bowl, cream the butter; add the sugar and eggs. Mix well. Then add the remaining ingredients, and mix. Pour into a pie plate lined with an unbaked pie crust. Bake for 1 hour or until the crust turns golden brown.

●● Eat up—and don't worry if you make a mess. To remove pie stains, see page 26.

epilogue

Hard work makes you healthy

When I asked Betty why she still spends her time working so hard at doing my family's laundry (and other people's laundry, as well) at age 76, she replied with certainty, "If I didn't like it, I wouldn't do it. Plus, the work keeps me healthy. Sometimes after a full day of laundry, I go out and walk 3 miles."

Betty rushes around at full speed all day long, sweating when it's blisteringly hot outside and hanging laundry on the clothesline in a T-shirt when it's freezing. When I look at her I can't help thinking, "They don't make people like they used to." I admire Betty's energy, her persistence, and her pride in her work. And I love—and am grateful for—the way she does laundry!

You may get discouraged and find yourself wondering if you'll ever be able to master the basic laundry techniques the way Betty has, but take heart in her time-tested wisdom. "I learn as I go along," she says, and she learns more every single day, and with every load of wash. With *Betty's Book of Laundry Secrets* and a small dose of perseverance, sock by dirty sock, you'll master the secrets of doing laundry well and enjoying it, too.

green laundry products

It's important to be kind to the Earth even when washing clothes. You can find petroleum-free laundry products at health food stores, a few grocery stores, and through the following catalogs and Web sites. So think green and stay clean!

Abundant Earth
762 West Park Avenue
Port Townsend, WA 98368
Phone: (360) 385-2186
Fax: (360) 385-2196
Web site:
    www.abundantearth.com

Cal Ben Soap Company
9828 Pearmain Street
Oakland, CA 94603
Phone: (800) 340-7091
Fax: (510) 638-STAR
    (510-638-7827)
Web site:
    www.CalBenPureSoap.com

Dr. Bronner's Magic Soaps
PO Box 28
Escondido, CA 92033
Phone: (760) 743-2211

Gaiam, Inc.
360 Interlocken Boulevard, Suite 300
Broomfield, CO 80021
Phone: (303) 464-3600
Fax: (303) 464-3700
Web site:
    www.gaiam.com

GreenMarketplace.com

5808 Forbes Avenue,
  2nd floor
Pittsburgh, PA 15217
Phone: (888) 59-EARTH
        (888-593-2784)
Fax: (412) 420-6404
Web site:
  www.greenmarketplace.com

Kokopelli's Green Market

PO Box 1899
Broomfield, CO
  80038-1899
Phone: (800) 210-0202
Fax: (303) 404-2008
Web site:
  www.kokopelliltd.com

Real Goods

13771 S. Highway 101
Hopland, CA 95449
Phone: (800) 762-7325
Web site: www.realgoods.com

Seventh Generation

One Mill Street, Box A26
Burlington, VT
  05401-1530
Phone: (802) 658-3773
Fax: (802) 658-1771
Web site:
  www.seventhgen.com

Sodasan USA, Inc.

4500 Garden Brook Drive
Chico, CA 95973
Phone: (530) 332-9500
Fax: (530) 332-9600

Sun and Earth

125 Noble Street
Norristown, PA 19401
Phone: (800) 596-7233
Fax: (610) 239-9688
Web site:
www.sunandearth.com

index

Note: Page references in *italic* indicate boxed text and tables. **Boldface** references indicate illustrations.

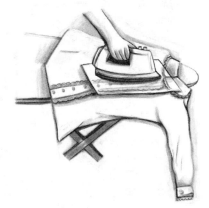